THE WINTER'S TALE

Shakespeare The Animated Tales is a multinational venture conceived by S4C, Channel 4 Wales. Produced in Russia, Wales and England, the series has been financed by S4C and the BBC (UK), Christmas Films (Russia), Home Box Office (USA) and Fujisankei (Japan).

Academic Panel
Professor Stanley Wells
Dr Rex Gibson

Educational Adviser
Michael Marland

Publishing Editor and Co-ordinator
Jane Fior

Book Design
Fiona Macmillan and Ness Wood

Animation Director for *The Winter's Tale*
Stanislav Sokolov of Christmas Films, Moscow

Series Editors
Martin Lamb and Penelope Middelboe, Right Angle, Tenby, Wales

Executive Producers
Christopher Grace (S4C)
Elizabeth Babakhina (Christmas Films)

Associate Producer
Theresa Plummer Andrews (BBC)

First published in 1994
by William Heinemann Ltd
an imprint of Reed Consumer Books Ltd
Michelin House, 81 Fulham Road, London SW3 6RB
and Auckland, Melbourne, Singapore and Toronto
Copyright © Shakespeare Animated Films/Christmas Films 1994

ISBN 0 434 96782 3

A CIP catalogue record for this title is available
from the British Library

Printed and bound in the UK by BPC Paulton Books Limited

The publishers would like to thank Paul Cox
for the series logo illustration,
Carol Kemp for her calligraphy,
Theo Crosby for the use of his painting of the Globe,
and Rosa Fior and Celia Salisbury Jones
for their help on the books.

Shakespeare
THE ANIMATED TALES

THE WINTER'S TALE

ABRIDGED BY LEON GARFIELD

ILLUSTRATED BY

ELENA LIVANOVA

AND STANISLAV SOKOLOV

HEINEMANN YOUNG BOOKS

William Shakespeare

Martin Droeshout sculpsit London.

WILLIAM SHAKESPEARE

NEXT TO GOD, A wise man once said, Shakespeare created most. In the thirty-seven plays that are his chief legacy to the world – and surely no-one ever left a richer! – human nature is displayed in all its astonishing variety.

He has enriched the stage with matchless comedies, tragedies, histories, and, towards the end of his life, with plays that defy all description, strange plays that haunt the imagination like visions.

His range is enormous: kings and queens, priests, princes and merchants, soldiers, clowns and drunkards, murderers, pimps, whores, fairies, monsters and pale, avenging ghosts 'strut and fret their hour upon the stage'. Murders and suicides abound; swords flash, blood flows, poison drips, and lovers sigh; yet there is always time for old men to talk of growing apples and for gardeners to discuss the weather.

In the four hundred years since they were written, they have become known and loved in every land; they are no longer the property of one country and one people, they are the priceless possession of the world.

His life, from what we know of it, was not astonishing. The stories that have attached themselves to him are remarkable only for their ordinariness: poaching deer, sleeping off a drinking bout under a wayside tree. There are no duels, no loud, passionate loves, no excesses of any kind. He was not one of your unruly geniuses whose habits are more interesting than their works. From all accounts, he was of a gentle, honourable disposition, a good businessman, and a careful father.

He was born on April 23rd 1564, to John and Mary Shakespeare of Henley Street, Stratford-upon-Avon. He was their third child and first son. When he was four or five he began his education at the local petty school. He left the local grammar school when he was about fourteen, in all probability to help in his father's glove-making shop. When he was eighteen, he married Anne Hathaway, who lived in a nearby village. By the time he was twenty-one, he was the father of three children, two daughters and a son.

Then, it seems, a restless mood came upon him. Maybe he travelled, maybe he was, as some say, a schoolmaster in the country; but at some time during the next seven years, he went to London and found employment in the theatre. When he was twenty-eight, he was already well enough known as an actor and playwright to excite the spiteful envy of a rival, who referred to him as 'an upstart crow'.

He mostly lived and worked in London until his mid-forties, when he returned to his family and home in Stratford, where he remained in prosperous circumstances until his death on April 23rd 1616, his fifty-second birthday.

He left behind him a widow, two daughters (his son died in childhood), and the richest imaginary world ever created by the human mind.

LEON GARFIELD

The list of the plays contained in the First Folio of 1623. This was the first collected edition of Shakespeare's plays and was gathered together by two of his fellow actors, John Hemmings and Henry Condell.

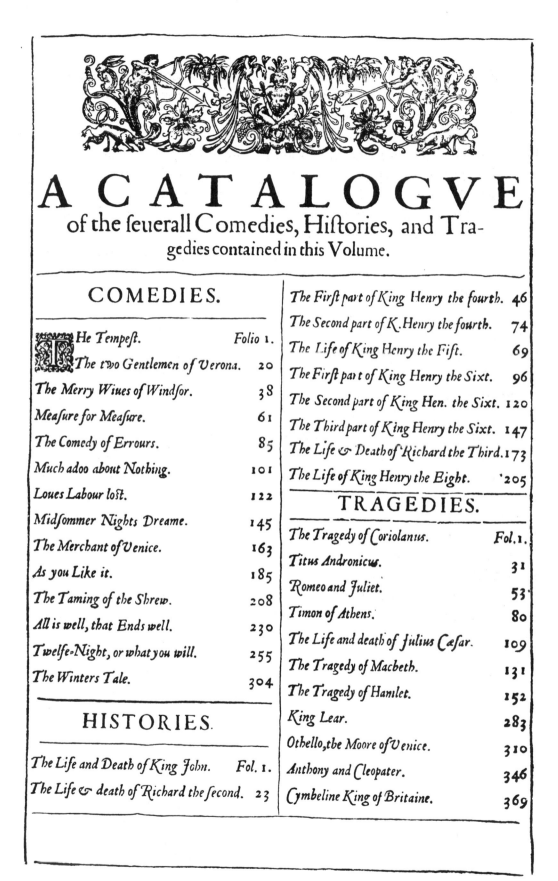

A CATALOGVE

of the feuerall Comedies, Hiftories, and Tragedies contained in this Volume.

THE THEATRE IN SHAKESPEARE'S DAY

IN 1989 AN ARCHAEOLOGICAL discovery was made on the south bank of the Thames that sent shivers of delight through the theatre world. A fragment of Shakespeare's own theatre, the Globe, where many of his plays were first performed, had been found.

This discovery has fuelled further interest in how Shakespeare himself conceived and staged his plays. We know a good deal already, and archaeology as well as documentary research will no doubt reveal more, but although we can only speculate on some of the details, we have a good idea of what the Elizabethan theatre-goer saw, heard and smelt when he went to see a play by William Shakespeare at the Globe.

It was an entirely different experience from anything we know today. Modern theatres have roofs to keep out the weather. If it rained on the Globe, forty per cent of the play-goers got wet. Audiences today sit on cushioned seats, and usually (especially if the play is by Shakespeare) watch and listen in respectful silence. In the Globe, the floor of the theatre was packed with a riotous crowd of garlic-reeking apprentices, house servants and artisans, who had each paid a penny to stand for the entire duration of the play, to buy nuts and apples from the food-sellers, to refresh themselves with bottled ale, relieve themselves, perhaps, into buckets by the back wall, to talk, cheer, catcall, clap and hiss if the play did not please them.

In the galleries that rose in curved tiers around the inside of the building sat those who could afford to pay two pennies for a seat, and the benefits of a roof over their heads. Here, the middle ranking citizens, the merchants, the sea captains, the clerks from the Inns of Court, would sit crammed into their small eighteen inch space and look down upon the 'groundlings' below. In the 'Lords' room', the rich and the great, noblemen and women, courtiers and foreign ambassadors had to pay sixpence each for the relative comfort and luxury of their exclusive position directly above the stage, where they smoked tobacco, and overlooked the rest.

We are used to a stage behind an arch, with wings on either side, from which the actors come on and into which they disappear. In the Globe, the stage was a platform thrusting out into the middle of the floor, and the audience, standing in the central yard, surrounded it on three sides. There were no wings. Three doors at the back of the stage were used for all exits and entrances. These were sometimes covered by a curtain, which could be used as a prop.

Today we sit in a darkened theatre or cinema, and look at a brilliantly lit stage or screen, or we sit at home in a small, private world of our own, watching a luminous television screen. The close-packed, rowdy crowd at the Globe, where the play started at two o'clock in the afternoon, had no artificial light to enhance their illusion. It was the words that moved them. They came to listen, rather than to see.

No dimming lights announced the start of the play. A blast from a trumpet and three sharp knocks warned the audience that the action was about to begin. In the broad daylight, the actor could see the audience as clearly as the audience could see him. He spoke directly to the crowd, and held them with his eyes, following their reactions. He could play up to the raucous laughter that greeted the comical, bawdy scenes, and gauge the emotional response to the higher flights of poetry. Sometimes he even improvised speeches of his own. He was surrounded by, enfolded by, his audience.

The stage itself would seem uncompromisingly bare to our eyes. There was no scenery. No painted backdrops suggested a forest, or a castle, or the sumptuous interior of a palace. Shakespeare painted the scenery with his words, and the imagination of the audience did the rest.

Props were brought onto the stage only when they were essential for the action. A bed would be carried on when a character needed to lie on it. A throne would be let down from above when a king needed to sit on it. Torches and lanterns would suggest that it was dark, but the main burden of persuading an audience, at three o'clock in the afternoon, that it was in fact the middle of the night, fell upon the language.

In our day, costume designers create a concept as part of the production of a play into which each costume fits. Shakespeare's actors were responsible for their own costumes. They would use what was to hand in the 'tiring house' (dressing room), or supplement it out of their own pockets. Classical, medieval and Tudor clothes could easily appear side by side in the same play.

No women actors appeared on a public stage until many years after

The Workes of William Shakeſpeare,

containing all his Comedies, Hiſtories, and
Tragedies: Truely ſet forth, according to their firſt
O R J G J N A L L.

The Names of the Principall Actors
in all theſe Playes.

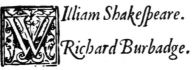

Illiam Shakeſpeare.

Richard Burbadge.

John Hemmings.

Auguſtine Phillips.

William Kempt.

Thomas Poope.

George Bryan.

Henry Condell.

William Slye.

Richard Cowly.

John Lowine.

Samuell Croſſe.

Alexander Cooke.

Samuel Gilburne.

Robert Armin.

William Oſtler.

Nathan Field.

John Vnderwood.

Nicholas Tooley.

William Eccleſtone.

Joſeph Taylor.

Robert Benfield.

Robert Goughe.

Richard Robinſon.

Iohn Shancke.

Iohn Rice.

Shakespeare's death, for at that time it would have been considered shameless. The parts of young girls were played by boys. The parts of older women were played by older men.

In 1613 the Globe theatre was set on fire by a spark from a cannon during a performance of Henry VIII, and it burnt to the ground. The actors, including Shakespeare himself, dug into their own pockets and paid for it to be rebuilt. The new theatre lasted until 1642, when it closed again. Now, in the 1990s, the Globe is set to rise again as a committed band of actors, scholars and enthusiasts are raising the money to rebuild Shakespeare's theatre in its original form a few yards from its previous site.

From the time when the first Globe theatre was built until today, Shakespeare's plays have been performed in a vast variety of languages, styles, costumes and techniques, on stage, on film, on television and in animated film. Shakespeare himself, working within the round wooden walls of his theatre, would have been astonished by it all.

PATRICK SPOTTISWOODE
Director of Education,
Globe Theatre Museum

From this list of actors, we can see that William Shakespeare not only wrote plays but also acted in them. The Globe theatre, where these actors performed, is now being rebuilt close to its original site on the south bank of the river Thames.

SHAKESPEARE TODAY

SHAKESPEARE IS ALIVE TODAY! Although William Shakespeare the man lies long buried in Stratford-upon-Avon parish church, he lives on in countless millions of hearts and minds.

Imagine that cold April day in 1616. The small funeral procession labours slowly along Church Street. Huge black horses draw the wooden cart bearing the simple coffin. On the coffin, a few daffodils and primroses, plucked only minutes before from the garden of New Place, gravely nod with each jolt and jar of the rutted road.

Most of Stratford's citizens have turned out, muffled against the biting wind, to see the last appearance of their wealthy neighbour. You couldn't call it a crowd. Just small respectful groups clustering the dry places on the roadside, careful to avoid the mud splashed up by the great hooves of the lumbering horses.

Men and women briefly bow their heads as the dead man and the black-clad mourners pass. The townspeople share their opinions, as neighbours do. "He used to do some acting, didn't he?" "Made a lot of money in London. Writing plays, I think." "Used to come home once a year to see his family, but nobody here really knew a lot about Master Shakespeare." "Wasn't he a poet?" "Big landowner hereabouts anyway. All those fields over at Welcombe."

Past the Guild Chapel where he had worshipped as a boy. Past the school where long ago his imagination was fired by language. At the churchyard gate, under the sad elms, six men effortlessly heave the coffin on to their shoulders. William Shakespeare is about to enter his parish church for the last time.

Nobody at that long ago funeral guessed that they were saying goodbye to a man who would become the most famous Englishman of his age – perhaps of all time.

Shakespeare lives on. He weaves familiar themes into his tales: the conflicts between parents and children, love at first sight, the power struggles of war and politics. His language is heard everywhere. If you ever call someone 'a blinking idiot' or 'a tower of strength', or describe them as 'tongue-tied', or suffering from 'green-eyed jealousy', or being 'dead as a doornail', you are speaking the language of Shakespeare.

If you say 'it was Greek to me' or 'parting is such sweet sorrow', or that something is 'too much of a good thing' and that you 'have not slept one wink', the words of Shakespeare are alive in your mouth. Shakespeare's language has a power all of its own, rich in emotional intensity. Because he was a poet who wrote plays, he could make even the simplest words utterly memorable. All around the world people know Hamlet's line 'To be or not to be, that is the question.'

Shakespeare is still performed today because of the electrifying power of his storytelling. Whether his story is about love or murder, or kings and queens, he keeps you on the edge of your seat wanting to know what happens next.

He created well over nine hundred characters in his plays. However large or small the part, each character springs vividly to life in performance. They live in our imagination because they are so much like people today. They experience the same emotions that everyone feels and recognises: love, jealousy, fear, courage, ambition, pride … and a hundred others.

In every play, Shakespeare invites us to imagine what the characters are like, and for nearly four hundred years people have accepted Shakespeare's invitation. The plays have been re-imagined in very many ways. They have been shortened, added to, and set in very different periods of history. They have been translated into many languages and performed all over the world. Shakespeare lives because all persons in every age and every society can make their own interpretations and performances of Shakespeare.

The creators of *The Animated Tales* have re-imagined *The Winter's Tale* in a 26 minute animated film. You too can make your own living Shakespeare. Read the text that follows, and watch the video. Then try reading the play either by yourself, changing your voice to suit the different characters, or with friends, and record it on a tape recorder. If you have a toy theatre, try staging it with characters and scenery that you make and paint yourself. Or collect together a cast and create your own production for your family and friends.

DR REX GIBSON

Dr Rex Gibson is the director of the Shakespeare and Schools Project which is part of the Institute of Education at the University of Cambridge.

In 1994 he was awarded the Sam Wanamaker International Shakespeare Award for his outstanding contribution to the world's knowledge of the works of Shakespeare.

WHAT THEY SAID OF HIM

One will ever find, in searching his works, new cause for astonishment and admiration.

GOETHE

Shakespeare was a writer of all others the most calculated to make his readers better as well as wiser.

SAMUEL TAYLOR COLERIDGE

An overstrained enthusiasm is more pardonable with respect to Shakespeare than the want of it; for our admiration cannot easily surpass his genius.

WILLIAM HAZLITT

It required three hundred years for England to begin to hear those two words that the whole world cries in her ear – William Shakespeare.

VICTOR HUGO

He has left nothing to be said about nothing or anything.

JOHN KEATS

The stream of time, which is continually washing the dissoluble fabrics of other poets, passes without injury by the adamant of Shakespeare.

SAMUEL JOHNSON

THE WINTER'S TALE

To my mind, of all Shakespeare's plays, *The Winter's Tale* is the most moving and the most magical. It is the story of King Leontes of Sicily, who, in a fit of mad jealousy, brings about the death of his beloved little son and his gracious queen, and causes his baby daughter to be carried away to some wild and savage place, and there left to the mercy of the elements. It is the story of that little daughter and what becomes of her; and of the old shepherd who finds her and brings her up as his own, not knowing she is a princess until —

The first part of the play is all terror and darkness; the second, all laughter and light. "Thou met'st with things dying," says the old shepherd to his son who has come to tell him of a man being eaten by a bear; "and I with things new-born," he says, and shows him the babe.

LEON GARFIELD

THE CHARACTERS IN THE PLAY

in order of appearance

LEONTES	*King of Sicilia*
MAMILLIUS	*young Prince of Sicilia*
CAMILLO	*a Lord of Sicilia*
POLIXENES	*King of Bohemia*
HERMIONE	*Queen to Leontes*
ANTIGONUS	*a Lord of Sicilia*
SERVANT	*to Leontes*
PAULINA	*wife to Antigonus*
A LORD	
A JUDGE	
AN OLD SHEPHERD	
THE OLD SHEPHERD'S SON	
TIME	
AUTOLYCUS	*a rogue*
PERDITA	*daughter to Leontes and Hermione*
FLORIZEL	*Prince of Bohemia, son of Polixenes*
FOUR GENTLEMEN	

Other ladies and gentlemen, servants, shepherds and shepherdesses

On a terrible day, a sudden madness strikes down Leontes, the king of Sicilia. In the twinkling of an eye, it turns him against those he loves best: Hermione, his queen, and Polixenes, king of Bohemia, his childhood friend and guest. He becomes convinced they are lovers and Polixenes the father of Hermione's unborn child.

The curtain rises on the palace of Leontes. It is winter. Polixenes and Hermione walk together. Leontes watches from a little distance, his arm about the shoulders of Mamillius, his little son.

LEONTES   Too hot, too hot! To mingle friendship far is mingling bloods. I have tremor cordis on me; my heart dances, but not for joy – not joy. Go play, boy, play. Thy mother plays, and I play too, but so disgrac'd a part. How now, boy? What! Hast smutched thy nose? They say it is a copy out of mine. Come, captain, we must be neat. (*He wipes his nose.*)

MAMILLIUS   I am like you, they say.

LEONTES   Why, that's some comfort. Go play, Mamillius.

Mamillius leaves.

LEONTES   What! Camillo there?

CAMILLO   Ay, my good lord.

LEONTES   Ha' not you seen, Camillo – but that's past doubt – that my wife is slippery?

CAMILLO   You never spoke what did become you less than this!

LEONTES   Is whispering nothing? Is leaning cheek to cheek? Kissing with inside lip? Is this nothing?

CAMILLO   Good my lord, be cur'd of this diseas'd opinion, and betimes, for 'tis most dangerous.

LEONTES   Say it be, 'tis true.

CAMILLO   No, no, my lord!

LEONTES   It is: you lie. Might'st bespice a cup to give mine enemy a lasting wink?

Leontes departs.

CAMILLO   What case stand I in? I must be the poisoner of good Polixenes.

Polixenes enters.

POLIXENES   The king hath on him such a countenance as he had lost some province. What is breeding that changes thus his manners?

CAMILLO   Sir, I will tell you – I am appointed him to murder you.

POLIXENES   By whom, Camillo?

CAMILLO   By the king.

POLIXENES   For what?

CAMILLO   He thinks, nay, with all confidence he swears, that you have touch'd his queen forbiddenly.

POLIXENES   O then, my best blood turn to an infected jelly! How should this grow?

CAMILLO   I know not; but I am sure 'tis safer to avoid what's grown than question how 'tis born. For myself, I'll put my fortunes to your service, which are here by this discovery lost.

POLIXENES   I do believe thee: I saw his heart in's face. Give me thy hand. My ships are ready.

In the queen's apartment, Hermione is with her ladies who are playing with little Mamillius.

HERMIONE   Come, sir, pray you sit by us, and tell's a tale.

MAMILLIUS   Merry, or sad, shall't be?

HERMIONE   As merry as you will.

MAMILLIUS   A sad tale's best for winter. I have one of sprites and goblins.

HERMIONE   Sit down, and do your best to fright me with your sprites.

MAMILLIUS   There was a man – dwelt by a churchyard . . .

Leontes and lords enter.

LEONTES   Bear the boy hence, he shall not come about her.

HERMIONE   What is this? Sport?

LEONTES   Away with him! And let her sport herself with that she's big with, for 'tis Polixenes has made thee swell thus. She's an adultress! (*The child is removed.*)

HERMIONE   Should a villain say so, the most replenish'd villain in the world, he were as much more villain: you, my lord, do but mistake.

LEONTES   You have mistook, my lady, Polixenes for Leontes. Away with her, to prison!

HERMIONE   Adieu, my lord, I never wish'd to see you sorry; now I trust I shall.

The queen departs under guard. Her ladies are in tears but she does not cry and gestures to them to be brave as she passes. Antigonus, an old nobleman, speaks up for her.

ANTIGONUS   I dare my life lay down that the queen is spotless.

LEONTES   Cease, no more. You smell this business with a sense as cold as is a dead man's nose; but I do see't and feel't. I have dispatch'd to sacred Delphos, to Apollo's temple. Though I am satisfied, yet shall the Oracle give rest to th'minds of others – such as he. (*He points to Antigonus.*)

Mamillius has fallen sick and a servant brings news of the child's condition to Leontes.

LEONTES   How does the boy?

SERVANT   He took good rest tonight; 'tis hop'd his sickness is discharg'd.

LEONTES   Go, see how he fares.

Hermione, in prison, has given birth to an infant girl. Her good friend, Paulina, wife of Antigonus, decides to take the baby to Leontes in the hope of curing him of his madness. But when she attempts to gain audience with Leontes, he is outraged.

LEONTES   Away with that audacious lady! Antigonus, I charg'd thee that she should not come about me. Canst not rule her?

ANTIGONUS   Hang all the husbands that cannot do that feat, you'll leave yourself hardly one subject.

PAULINA   Good my liege, I come from your good queen.

LEONTES   Good queen?

PAULINA   The good queen – for she is good – hath brought you forth a daughter, here 'tis.

LEONTES A mankind witch! Hence with her, out o' door! Give her the bastard, thou dotard! Tak't up, I say: give it to thy crone!

Antigonus stands frozen.

LEONTES He dreads his wife. This brat is none of mine.

PAULINA It is yours: and so like you, 'tis the worse.

LEONTES I'll have thee burnt!

PAULINA I care not.

LEONTES Out of the chamber with her!

PAULINA I'll be gone. Look to your babe, my lord, 'tis yours.

She departs, leaving the child to its father's mercy.

LEONTES Thou, traitor, hast set on thy wife to this. My child? Away with't! Go, take it to the fire.

LORD Beseech your highness, on our knees we beg that you do change this purpose, which, being so horrible, so bloody, must lead on to some foul issue.

They kneel.

LEONTES   Be it: let it live. What will you adventure to save this brat's life?

ANTIGONUS   Any thing, my lord.

LEONTES   Mark, and perform it. We enjoin thee that thou carry this female bastard hence, and that thou bear it to some remote and desert place, quite out of our dominions; and that there thou leave it to its own protection: take it up.

ANTIGONUS   Come on, poor babe: some powerful spirit instruct the kites and ravens to be thy nurses.

Antigonus takes up the babe and hastens away.

SERVANT   Please your highness, posts from those you sent to the Oracle are come.

LEONTES   Prepare you, my lords, summon a session that we may arraign our most disloyal lady.

In the place of justice, Hermione stands before her accuser.

JUDGE   Hermione, queen to the worthy Leontes, king of Sicilia, thou art here accused and arraigned of high treason, in committing adultery with Polixenes, king of Bohemia.

HERMIONE   You, my lord, best know my past life hath been as continent, as chaste, as true, as I am now unhappy. Your honours, I do refer me to the Oracle: Apollo be my judge!

LORD   This your request is altogether just.

The officers go to fetch the messengers.

HERMIONE   The Emperor of Russia was my father. O that he were alive, and here beholding his daughter's trial! That he did but see the flatness of my misery, yet with eyes of pity, not revenge.

The officers return with the two messengers.

LEONTES   Break up the seals and read.

JUDGE   (*reading*) Hermione is chaste; Polixenes blameless; Camillo a true subject; Leontes a jealous tyrant; his innocent babe truly begotten; and the king shall live without an heir, if that which is lost be not found.

LORDS   Now blessed be the great Apollo.

LEONTES   There is no truth at all in the Oracle!

There is a clap of thunder. A servant rushes in.

LEONTES   The sessions shall proceed: this is mere falsehood.

SERVANT   My lord the king! Your son is gone!

LEONTES   How? Gone?

SERVANT   Is dead.

Leontes stares in horror at what his madness has brought about.

LEONTES   Apollo's angry, and the heavens themselves do strike at my injustice!

Hermione swoons. She is carried away by her ladies with Paulina in tearful attendance.

PAULINA   This news is mortal to the queen. Look down and see what death is doing.

LEONTES   Take her hence. Beseech you, tenderly apply to her some remedies for life. I'll reconcile me to Polixenes, new woo my queen, recall the good Camillo. How his piety does my deeds make the blacker!

Paulina returns.

PAULINA   The queen! The sweet'st, dear'st creature's dead! O thou
            tyrant! Betake thee to nothing but despair.

LEONTES   Go on, go on: I have deserv'd all tongues to talk their bitt'rest.
            Prithee bring me to the dead bodies of my queen and son; one
            grave shall be for both: upon them shall the causes of their
            deaths appear, unto our shame perpetual.

*Antigonus, obeying his master's harsh command, takes the
babe and sets sail from Sicilia. On board ship, Antigonus has a
strange vision in which Hermione appears before him. Such is
the nature of the vision that Antigonus is convinced of
Hermione's guilt.*

HERMIONE   Good Antigonus, since fate hath made thy person for the
            thrower-out of my poor babe, places remote enough are in
            Bohemia, there weep, and leave it crying; and, for the babe is
            counted lost forever, Perdita, I prithee call it.

            *Antigonus, having landed on the rocky sea coast of Bohemia in
            the midst of a terrible storm, leaves the child to its fate.*

ANTIGONUS   Blossom, speed thee well. There lie, and there thy character.

            He places a box and bundle of possessions beside the baby.

ANTIGONUS   Farewell, the day frowns more and more: thou'rt like to have a lullaby too rough. (*A bear appears.*) I am gone forever! (*Exit, pursued by a bear.*)

The storm increases in fury and overwhelms the waiting ship. Meanwhile, a shepherd searching for lost sheep, comes upon the babe.

SHEPHERD   What have we here? Mercy on's, a barne? I'll take it up for pity: yet I'll tarry till my son come. Ahoa!

An answering shout. Enter the shepherd's son.

SON   I have seen two such sights, by sea and land!

SHEPHERD   Why boy, how is it?

In answer to the shepherd's question, the son tells how he saw all the sailors drowned and Antigonus eaten by the bear.

SHEPHERD   Now bless thyself: thou met'st with things dying, I with things new born. Here's a sight for thee: look thee, a bearing-cloth for a squire's child. Look thee here, take up, boy, open it. What's within, boy?

His son opens the box and finds Hermione's jewels.

SON   You're a made old man! Gold! All gold!

SHEPHERD   This is fairy gold, and 'twill prove so. 'Tis a lucky day, boy, and we'll do good deeds on't.

The sky lightens and across the landscape of Bohemia a strange spectre strides: a pale figure bearing an hourglass. It is Time.

TIME   In the name of Time, I slide over sixteen years. In fair Bohemia, a son of the king's which Florizel I now name to you. And Perdita now grown in grace, a shepherd's daughter.

In the royal palace, Polixenes and Camillo stand together, gazing out of the window. It is high summer.

POLIXENES Say to me, when sawest thou the Prince Florizel, my son?

CAMILLO Sir, it is three days since I saw the prince.

POLIXENES I have this intelligence, that he is seldom from the house of a most homely shepherd: a man, they say, that from very nothing, is grown into an unspeakable estate.

CAMILLO I have heard, sir, of such a man, who hath a daughter of most rare note.

POLIXENES Thou shalt accompany us to the place.

CAMILLO I obey your command.

POLIXENES My best Camillo! We must disguise ourselves.

On a country road, a lively figure appears. It is Autolycus, a cheerful pilferer of everything that has not been nailed down.

AUTOLYCUS (*singing*) When daffodils begin to peer,
 With heigh the doxy over the dale,
 Why then comes in the sweet o' the year.
 For the red blood reigns in the winter's pale.

My father named me Autolycus, who was likewise a snapper-up of unconsidered trifles. (*He sees the shepherd's son approaching.*) A prize, a prize!

SON   Let me see, what am I to buy for our sheep-shearing feast? Three pound of sugar, five pound of currants, rice: what will this sister of mine do with rice? But my father hath made her Mistress of the Feast –

Autolycus flings himself in the son's path, wailing and moaning.

AUTOLYCUS   O help me, help me! I am robbed, sir, and beaten.

SON   Lend me thy hand, I'll help thee.

AUTOLYCUS   O good sir, tenderly, oh!

As the son helps Autolycus to his feet, his pocket is skilfully picked.

SON   How now? Canst stand? Dost lack any money? I have a little money for thee.

AUTOLYCUS   No, good sweet sir! Offer me no money, I pray you; that kills my heart.

SON   Then fare thee well, I must go buy spices for our sheep-shearing.

The son departs.

AUTOLYCUS   (*examining his booty*) Prosper you, sweet sir. I'll be with you at your sheep-shearing too. (*He sets off along the road, singing.*)

> Jog on, jog on, the footpath way,
> And merrily hent the stile-a:
> A merry heart goes all the day.
> Your sad tires in a mile-a.

Before the shepherd's cottage, everything is in readiness for the sheep-shearing. There is music and dancing and Perdita, attired as Queen of the Feast, speaks to Florizel who is dressed as a very grand shepherd.

She moves away from Florizel and gives flowers and herbs to Polixenes and Camillo who are strangers at the feast.

PERDITA   Reverend sirs, for you, there's rosemary and rue; grace and remembrance be to you both, and welcome to our sheep-shearing.

Florizel returns to her side.

FLORIZEL   Come, our dance I pray, your hand, my Perdita.

He leads her off and they join the dance.

POLIXENES   This is the prettiest low-born lass, that ever ran on greensward.

CAMILLO   Good sooth, she is the queen of curds and cream!

POLIXENES   Pray good shepherd, what fair swain is this, which dances with your daughter?

SHEPHERD   They call him Doricles. He says he loves my daughter: I think so too. I think there is not half a kiss to choose who loves another best. (*Autolycus enters, singing.*)

AUTOLYCUS
                                    Will you buy any tape,
                                    Or lace for your cape,
                                    My dainty duck, my dear-a?
                                    Any silk, any thread,
                                    Any toys for your head . . .
                                    Of the new'st, and fin'st, wear-a?

The dancers eagerly stream after him. Perdita and Florizel are left. Polixenes beckons them near.

POLIXENES   Sooth, when I was young, and handed love, as you do, I was wont to load my she with knacks; I would have ransack'd the pedlar's silken treasury —

FLORIZEL   (*with dramatic sincerity*) Old sir, I know she prizes not such trifles as these are. The gifts she looks from me, are pack'd and lock'd up in my heart, which I have given already, but not delivered.

SHEPHERD   Take hands, a bargain; and friends unknown, you shall bear witness to't: I give my daughter to him, and will make her portion equal his. Come, your hand: and daughter, yours.

POLIXENES   Soft, swain, awhile, beseech you. Have you a father?

FLORIZEL   I have: but what of him?

POLIXENES   Knows he of this?

FLORIZEL   He neither does, nor shall.

POLIXENES   By my white beard, you offer him a wrong something unfilial. Let him know't.

FLORIZEL   He shall not: mark our contract.

POLIXENES (*revealing himself*) Mark your divorce, young sir, whom son I
dare not call: thou art too base to be acknowledged; thou a
sceptre's heir that thus affects a sheep-hook! Thou, old traitor,
I am sorry, that by hanging thee, I can but shorten thy life one
week. And thou, if ever henceforth thou hoop his body more
with thy embraces, I will devise a death, as cruel for thee as
thou art tender to't.

He storms away, leaving all aghast.

PERDITA   I was not much afeared: for once, or twice I was about to
speak, and tell him plainly, the self-same sun that shines upon
his court hides not his visage from our cottage, but looks on
alike. (*To Florizel*) Will't please you, sir, be gone?

SHEPHERD   O sir, you have undone a man of fourscore three. (*To Perdita*)
O cursed wretch, thou knew'st this was the prince! Undone,
undone! If I might die within this hour, I have lived to die when
I desire.

The old shepherd leaves.

FLORIZEL   (*to Camillo and Perdita*) Why look you so upon me? I am sorry, not afear'd: delay'd, but nothing alter'd: what I was, I am —

CAMILLO   Gracious my lord —

FLORIZEL   Camillo, not for Bohemia will I break my oath to this fair belov'd. This you may know, and so deliver, I am put to sea with her whom here I cannot hold on shore. I have a vessel rides fast by.

CAMILLO   This is desperate sir. Have you thought on a place whereto you'll go?

FLORIZEL   Not any yet.

CAMILLO   Then list to me. Make for Sicilia and there present yourself and your fair princess 'fore Leontes. (*Autolycus walks by.*) We'll make an instrument of this. How now, good fellow?

AUTOLYCUS   I am a poor fellow, sir.

CAMILLO   Why, be so still. Yet for the outside of thy poverty we must make an exchange: therefore discase thee instantly and change garments with this gentleman. There's some boot. (*Gives him money.*) What I do next shall be to tell the king of this escape to force him after.

The terrified shepherd and his son are on their way to the palace with the box and bundle of possessions that they found with the infant Perdita.

SON   There is no other way but to tell the king she's a changeling, and none of your flesh and blood.

SHEPHERD   I will tell the king all, every word, yea, and his son's pranks too. There is that in this fardel will make him scratch his beard. (*He taps the bundle.*)

Autolycus enters. He has overheard the last.

AUTOLYCUS   How now, rustics, whither are you bound?

SHEPHERD   To the palace, and it like your worship.

AUTOLYCUS   What's in the fardel? Wherefore that box?

SHEPHERD   Sir, there lies such secrets in this fardel and box which none must know but the king.

AUTOLYCUS   Age, thou hast lost thy labour. The king is not at the palace. He is gone aboard a new ship. I'll bring you where he is.

SON   He seems to be of great authority. Close with him, give him gold.

SHEPHERD   An't please you sir, to undertake the business for us, here is that gold I have.

AUTOLYCUS   Walk before, toward the sea-side. (*They walk on.*) If I had a mind to be honest, I see Fortune would not suffer me: she drops booties in my mouth. To the prince will I present them, there may be matter in it.

In Sicilia, Leontes still mourns the loss of his Hermione as does Paulina of her Antigonus. His lords try to persuade him to take another wife.

LORD   Sir, you have done enough, and have perform'd a saint-like sorrow.

PAULINA   You are one of those would have him wed again. There is none
            worthy, respecting her that's gone. Besides, has not the divine
            Apollo said that King Leontes shall not have an heir till his lost
            child be found?

LEONTES   My true Paulina, we shall not marry till thou bid'st us.

PAULINA   That shall be when your first queen's again in breath: never till
            then. (*As she speaks, a servant enters.*)

SERVANT   One that gives out himself Prince Florizel, son of Polixenes,
            with his princess – she the fairest I have yet beheld – desires
            access to your high presence.

LEONTES   He comes not like to his father's greatness. Bring them to our
            embracement. Still, 'tis strange he thus should steal upon us.

Florizel and Perdita enter.

LEONTES   Were I but twenty-one, your father's image is so hit in you – his very air – that I should call you brother. Welcome hither, as is the spring to th'earth.

A lord enters.

LORD   Please you, great sir, Polixenes greets you from himself by me; desires you to attach his son, who has fled from his father, from his hopes, and with a shepherd's daughter.

LEONTES   Where's Polixenes? Speak.

LORD   Here, in your city. To your court whiles he was hastening, meets he on the way the father of this seeming lady and her brother.

PERDITA   O my poor father!

LEONTES   (*to Florizel*) You are married?

FLORIZEL   We are not, sir, nor are we like to be.

LEONTES   My lord, is this the daughter of a king?

FLORIZEL   She is, when once she is my wife.

LEONTES   That 'once', I see, by your good father's speed, will come on very slowly.

FLORIZEL   Beseech you sir, step forth mine advocate. At your request, my father will grant precious things as trifles.

LEONTES   I will to your father. Come.

In Sicilia, church bells are ringing everywhere. The two kings have met. The old shepherd's box and bundle which contained the secrets of Perdita's birth have been opened. The Oracle has been fulfilled: the king's daughter has been found.

Autolycus and three gentlemen enter. A fourth approaches.

1ST GENTLEMAN   This news, which is so like an old tale: has the king found his heir?

3RD GENTLEMAN   Most true. Did you see the meeting of the two kings?

2ND GENTLEMAN	No.
3RD GENTLEMAN	Then have you lost a sight! Our king being ready to leap out of himself, for joy of his found daughter, cries 'O, thy mother, thy mother!' Then asks Polixenes forgiveness, then embraces his son-in-law, now he thanks the old shepherd.
4TH GENTLEMAN	The princess hearing of her mother's statue – which is in the keeping of Paulina – a piece many years in doing, by that rare Italian master, Julio Romano – thither are they gone.
1ST GENTLEMAN	Let's along.

They depart, leaving Autolycus. The old shepherd and his son approach. They are splendidly dressed.

AUTOLYCUS	Here come those I have done good to against my will. (*He bows to them.*) I humbly beseech you, sir, to pardon me all the faults I have committed.
SHEPHERD	Prithee, son, do: for we must be gentle, now we are gentlemen.
SON	Thou wilt amend thy life?
AUTOLYCUS	Ay, and it like your good worship.
SON	Come, follow us: we'll be thy good masters.

All are assembled in a chapel in Paulina's house. The statue of Hermione is hidden behind a curtain.

LEONTES   O Paulina, we came to see the statue of our queen.

PAULINA   Here it is. (*Draws back the curtain*). Comes it not something near?

LEONTES   Her natural posture. Chide me, dear stone, that I may say indeed thou art Hermione. But yet, Paulina, Hermione was not so much wrinkled, nothing so aged as this seems.

POLIXENES   Oh, not by much.

PAULINA   So much the more our carver's excellence, which lets go by some sixteen years, and makes her as she liv'd now.

LEONTES   As now she might have done. Oh royal piece, there's magic in thy majesty.

PERDITA   (*kneeling*) Lady, dear queen, that ended when I but began, give me that hand of yours, to kiss.

PAULINA   O patience: the statue is but newly fix'd; the colour's not dry.

LEONTES   Let no man mock me, for I will kiss her.

PAULINA   Good my lord, forbear; the ruddiness upon her lip is wet: you'll mar it if you kiss it. Shall I draw the curtain?

LEONTES   No: not these twenty years.

PERDITA   So long could I stand by, a looker-on.

PAULINA   If you can behold it, I'll make the statue move indeed; descend, and take you by the hand. It is requir'd you do awake your faith. Music, awake her; strike; 'tis time; descend; be stone no more; approach.

The statue descends. It is Hermione herself. She is alive and holds out her hands to Leontes.

PAULINA   When she was young, you woo'd her: now, in age, is she become the suitor?

LEONTES   (*taking Hermione's hand*) Oh she's warm! If this be magic, let it be an art lawful as eating.

Hermione embraces Leontes – silence descends as she hangs on his neck.

CAMILLO   If she pertain to life, let her speak too.

PAULINA   Mark a little while. (*To Perdita*) Please you to interpose, fair madam, kneel, and pray your mother's blessing; turn, good lady, our Perdita is found.

HERMIONE   (*crying, her tears falling as a heavenly blessing on her daughter*) You Gods look down, and from your sacred vials pour your graces upon my daughter's head! Tell me, mine own, where hast thou been preserv'd? where liv'd?

PAULINA   There's time enough for that. Go together, you precious winners all. I, an old turtle, will wing me to some wither'd bough, and there my mate, that's never to be found again, lament, till I am lost.

LEONTES   O peace, Paulina! Thou should'st a husband take by my consent, as I by thine a wife. Come, Camillo, and take her by the hand. Good Paulina, lead us from hence, where we may leisurely each one demand, and answer to his part perform'd in this wide gap of time, since first we were dissever'd.

The curtain falls.